Visual education in the primary school

JOHN M PICKERING

Visual education in the primary school

B T Batsford Limited   London
Watson-Guptill Publications   New York

© *John M Pickering 1971*
First published 1971
7134 2289 0
Watson-Guptill SBN *0 8230 6340 2*
Library of Congress Catalog
Card Number 79 114201

Filmset in Monophoto Ehrhardt, 12pt solid
by Filmtype Services Ltd, Scarborough, Yorks
Printed in Denmark by F E Bording Ltd, Copenhagen
Bound by Hunter & Foulis, Edinburgh
for the publishers
B T Batsford Ltd
4 Fitzhardinge Street, London W1 and
Watson-Guptill Publications
165 West 46th Street, New York, NY 10036

Contents

Acknowledgment

I am grateful to my wife and to all the teachers, students and children who contributed knowingly or unknowingly to this book and made it possible. My very special thanks must go to R. Wesley, Principal of Alsager College of Education, Cheshire, for his willing permission to use photographs of the work of students from the College, also to Edith Hully recently Head Mistress of Handforth Hall County Infants School, Cheadle, Cheshire and now Adviser for Primary Education in Suffolk who gave untold help and encouragement, to Pauline Watkin, Head Mistress of the Priory Church of England Infants School, Staffordshire, to Beryl Read, Head Mistress of Bosley St Mary's Church of England Primary School, to Lisa Lloyd of Langlands Infants School, Fife, and to Pamela Williams for invaluable secretarial assistance

The endpapers are a photogram of drawing pins (thumbtacks).

J M P
Alsager 1971

Introduction

There can be no one approach to the teaching of visual education. Art is by its nature dynamic and art teaching should be under constant review.

It would be pretentious to suggest that this book is any more than a primer in visual education in the primary school, although the area suggested can be explored by any age group. Its aim is to suggest possible ideas and it is hoped that these ideas will spark off fresh and exciting developments.

Art is a subject that is concerned essentially with seeing, education is concerned with understanding, visual education may be understood in its simplest terms, as a blending of the two. The most common present interpretation of art teaching, that has its roots in the 'Romantic' idealogical concepts of art education in the early part of the century, is to try to produce a state of complete freedom. If this is possible which is doubtful, it may have therapeutic value. Most young children need very little encouragement to invent and produce art products. Even very young children, being faced with paper and paint at a set time each day and then being asked to create pictures cannot produce any more than a development of technique which often leads to lack of interest.

A wide variety of learning situations are essential to maintain interest and inventiveness with the resultant growth and understanding. Situations in which a child cannot lean on preconceived ideas, and where intuitive thrusts are made into the unknown, are of immense educational value. The danger here may lie in that we pre-suppose the understanding of concepts, and it is here that the teacher can produce situations that are pleasurable and exciting, and that are designed to lead to discovering these concepts.

In this book areas for exploration are suggested and a logical progression of discovery is put forward, starting with the very simplest approach, that of sorting and using the curiosity of the child to discover the simple relationships that exist in the activities, materials and techniques presented.

Perhaps we are too often blinded by the very normality of what we see when we observe children at play. A child playing with a clockwork toy is playing with time, a child playing with bricks is playing with space, and a child stroking an animal is undergoing a tactile experience. Similarities are found in the scribble of a child, a fireworks explosion and a cobweb. All of these are diagrams of the movement and force that produced them.

A further attempt in this book has been made to relate the activities in the classroom to the world outside it. Frequently it is suggested that the children should get out and note what they see in their environment. The world abounds in colour, texture, and is space and the interruption of space. Our lives are entirely concerned with movement.

It is of the utmost importance that we take time to see and to register and not be constantly involved in the production of art products, even though they may give pleasure when displayed on parents' days, for unless they have been part of a sensitively directed and carefully considered situation, their value is likely to be superficial.

Much revolutionary reform is needed in the whole structure of the education system if visual education is to make its real contribution to the creative development of our children. Perhaps we have been guided too long by the carefully prepared charts or symbolic images produced by children at such-and-such an age.

Can we, with the immense wealth of psychological philosophical information and our own experiences to refer to, really believe that the safest way to approach visual education today is to do almost nothing?

VISUAL EDUCATION THROUGH THE AREAS
SUGGESTED IN THE FOLLOWING CHAPTERS

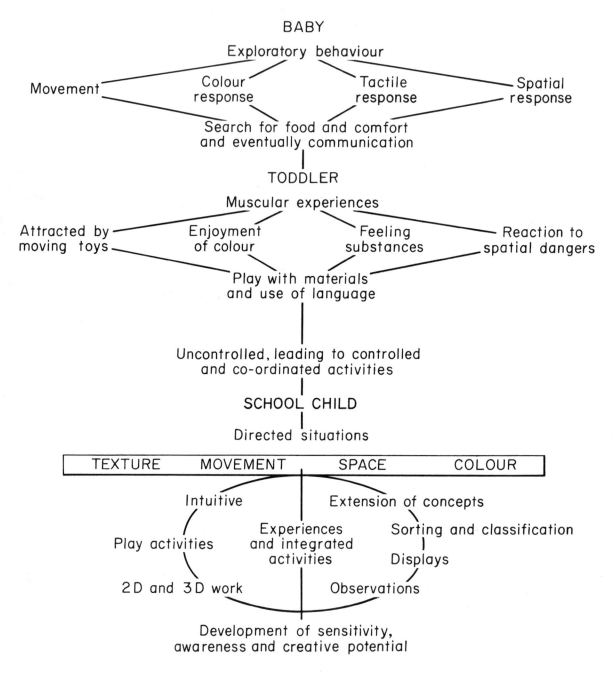

BABY

Exploratory behaviour

Movement   Colour response   Tactile response   Spatial response

Search for food and comfort
and eventually communication

TODDLER

Muscular experiences

Attracted by moving toys   Enjoyment of colour   Feeling substances   Reaction to spatial dangers

Play with materials
and use of language

Uncontrolled, leading to controlled
and co-ordinated activities

SCHOOL CHILD

Directed situations

TEXTURE   MOVEMENT   SPACE   COLOUR

Intuitive   Extension of concepts

Play activities   Experiences and integrated activities   Sorting and classification

Displays

2D and 3D work   Observations

Development of sensitivity,
awareness and creative potential

Part 1   Tactile and textural experiences

It is widely accepted that the early stages of a child's activity are concerned with physical experiments and experiences, which are closely related to muscular co-ordination. Perhaps the earliest sensations of pleasure and security are provided by the sense of touch.

In these stages the manipulation of materials is normally carried out with the fingers and hands. The substance, be it paint or jam, is pushed and smeared, and there can be little doubt that pleasure is derived from the experience. The understanding of the quality of a material is gained in two ways, by vision and by touch, confirmation normally coming about by feeling the surface. At this early stage, children experience the quality of surfaces by touch alone, but gradually, as they become older, they confirm by vision, until as adults they tend to reverse the process. Most adults see an object and confirm its substance by touching it. There is, however, a very strong relationship between the tactile and visual senses.

Most very young children enjoy the feel of a sticky substance or the feel of the wetness of spilt drink, the softness of a toy or the hardness of wood or metal. The mouth and cheek are the most sensitive parts of the body, and children will often test the feel of substances against their faces. They will nestle a kitten to their cheeks

1 *One of the earliest responses is provided by the sense of touch*

2   *Children love fondling the fur of animals;*
they enjoy the tactile experience

3   *Children often test the feel of substances*
against their faces

and touch things with their lips. At the seaside, everyone has seen children enjoying the sensation of playing with dry sand, allowing it to run through their fingers and toes, or seen the excitement of a child finding a beautiful, smooth pebble and feeling it in the palms of his hands.

This inherent sensitivity to the surface quali-ties of objects should stay with us for a lifetime, and does with many people, but, like drawing, it can die from neglect. Through considered teach-ing, the development of this ability can make children much more sensitive to the world in which they live, a world of textures, natural and man-made, random and contrived.

PLATE 1 *Controlled scribble*

Scribble and its development

The first marks that children make are done in a random manner. They are made through the exploration of touch, and gradually these marks, or scribbles, develop from the erratic state to one of control, and this control usually runs parallel to the development of muscular co-ordination. It is not uncommon for children to use either the left or right hand, or in fact both hands, to smear and daub the paint. The consistency of the media is important, and children tend to reject a consistency which they find difficult to manipulate. From these early erratic lines and daubs there usually emerges the use of vertical and horizontal lines, and a circular action is also very common. As the muscular co-ordination develops, so the tactile sensitivity tends to fade and the lines begin to emerge as shapes. The shapes are used to represent objects that exist within the limited world of the child and these shapes evolve as the child's knowledge increases. The basic shapes can be anything the child wishes them to be at a particular moment in time, from Mummy, to a car, to a spider, and the same shapes can be several things. Normally the use of lines is predominant, but the introduction of a new material can excite, and being unfamiliar to a child, he or she will often return to a tactile exploration of its substance.

4   Circular action in children's scribble is very common

13

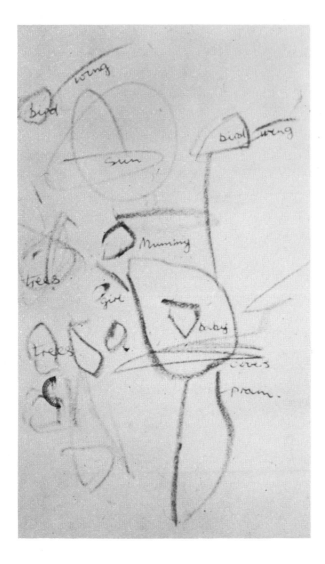

5 *Lines and an extremely limited number of shapes are used to present objects within the world of a child*

6 *Figures in a train, revealing only the dominant aspects*

7   *Man watering a garden, showing a
development of symbolic drawing and the
economy in using the same scheme to represent
the body and watering can*

Texture in the environment

The world is full of texture; texture in nature is abundant and varied, ranging in scale from the microscopic to the infinite. Qualities vary from the similar to the absolute opposite. Its form is organised or confused, from the even rhythm of the texture of the bark of a tree to wood eroded and eaten away by insects, or the action of water, wind, and sand, or force pressures of weight, thrust, twisting and tearing or cutting.

The textures of sand and water have an everlasting attraction for both children and adults and their potential for experimental play activities make them commonplace in the infant classroom, but more could be done to capitalise on this love of texture which is as basic as their love of drawing, music and dancing.

8 ABOVE *Frost on the window of a car produces exciting textures*

9 RIGHT *Texture created by sunlight on the sea; combining light and movement*

16

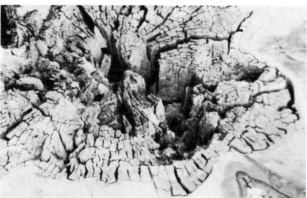
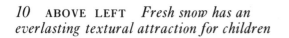

10 ABOVE LEFT *Fresh snow has an everlasting textural attraction for children*

11 BELOW LEFT *Rotting tree trunk very slowly changing its appearance day by day, year by year*

12 ABOVE RIGHT *Rusting scaffolding also undergoing very gradual change*

13 and 14 CENTRE RIGHT AND BELOW *Textures produced by tearing and cutting wood*

Man-made textures

Man produces textures that are contrived and textures that are random. Those that are contrived are normally of a decorative nature, for example the various finishes on houses, different kinds of frosted glass, wallpapers, fabrics, plastics and concrete. Texture can also have a functional application, and this is normally used to increase adhesion or friction, for example the tread on tyres, the knurled handles of tools and instruments, handlebar grips and pedals on a bicycle and the non-slip surfaces on roads and footpaths. The random textures usually occur by chance like the scattered bricks on a building site. Children should be encouraged to observe or record these groups of textures by rubbings, prints, drawings or photography.

TEXTURES MADE BY MAN BOTH RANDOM AND CONTRIVED

15 ABOVE *Pipes on a building site*

16 CENTRE *Water tower at York University*

17 BELOW *Reinforcing wire*

18   *Bricks in a random pattern*   19   *Tyre tread*

Sorting and understanding textural qualities

The collection of textural objects is a simple matter and usually children respond well to this kind of work, and a wide range of objects varying in size, shape and colour emerges from their enthusiasm. The problem of sorting really commences when the objects have been collected and some order has to be made from the chaotic array that results. This is normally most simply approached by sorting the objects into two piles: (1) man-made, and (2) natural. Sub-divisions of these can be made by selecting contrasting textural qualities, for example, rough/smooth, hard/soft, or qualities such as translucent/opaque, shiny/dull. Natural objects can be sub-divided into those which have had life and those which have never had life.

Extension of vocabulary

The choice of the adjectives used to describe the textures will depend very much upon the ages of the children who are required to use them. With the very young children, obviously the vocabulary should be kept as simple as possible. It is important that the various words describing the textures are understood, and a simple way to check this can be made by asking the children to place cards depicting the words chosen against the relevant objects.

Collections of photographs of things having pronounced textures could be suggested and work cards made to encourage children to search for both applied and natural textures in their environment. This written information could be supplemented by rubbings from surfaces like walls, tiles, wood or glass, etc., and, depending upon the ages of the children, more challenge could be induced by presenting certain limitations to their search. Peter Green's book on *Creative Print Making*, suggests many interesting extensions to this kind of search. Other three-dimensional work ranging from the pressures of textural objects into clay or plasticine, textures created by the addition and subtraction of clay, or the changing of the character of a surface by pin-pricking or cutting of paper or cardboard would be worthy of exploration. More sophisticated work can quite easily be incorporated in the pottery and sculpture of older children.

20   *Sorting stones and shells into rough and smooth groups*

Tactile experiment (Two-dimensional work
from touch experience)

A simple experiment was carried out by student
teachers at a primary school, which took the
following form. The children were asked to
make a collection of various objects and to sort
them into their two groups, natural and man-
made; cards were made stating the main charac-
teristics (rough, smooth, hard, soft, etc.) and a
display table was set up at the side of the classroom. Once the children had become familiar
with a simple vocabulary of words describing
textures, various objects were chosen for their
particular tactile qualities and hidden behind
curtains in the corner of the classroom. These
objects were quite new and unfamiliar to the
children and the children were encouraged to
push their hands through the slit in the curtains
and to feel the surfaces of the objects. They were
then asked to express what they had felt either in
two or three dimensions. The media chosen was
paint or clay. Quite astonishing results were ob-
tained and children used tone to represent weight
and dynamic shapes to symbolise hardness or
softness. In one particular case, colour was
blended to represent the softness of feathers.
Frequently lines or arrows were used to show the
kind of pressures or the directions of the pressures on a particular material. The symbols were
always of a highly personal nature and the children entered into the exercise without inhibitions,
and in fact with great enjoyment at this play with
a purpose.

21 ABOVE *Stage 1 of the experiment.*
Children being introduced to various objects. At
this stage the teacher is testing the vocabulary
and understanding of the children

22 RIGHT *Detail of sorting the various*
qualities of texture: sea urchin

23 ABOVE *Stage 2 Children in this stage were asked to feel objects without being able to see them*

24 LEFT *Detail of feeling*

25   *Stage 3 The interpretation of the unseen but felt objects. A sponge*

26   *A loofah*

27   *Concentric circles representing an object that was hard on the outside and soft in the centre*

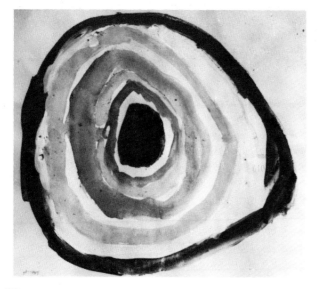

28   *A similar presentation by the same child showing an object that was hard on the outside and also in the centre*

26

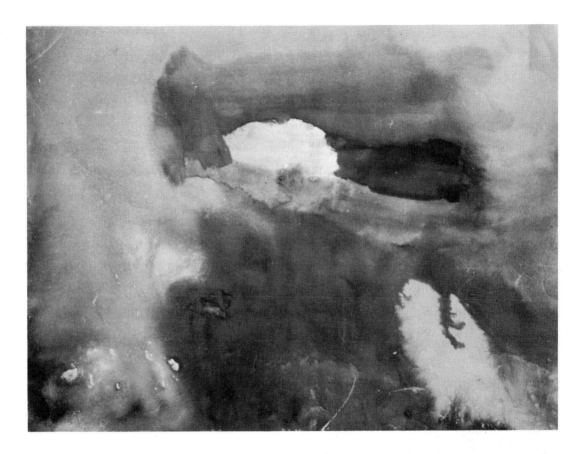

29 *Astonishing use of paint to represent the softness of feathers*

Sound

Sound, too, can be represented by texture, and with older children there may be advantages in exposing the children to a situation for which they are unlikely to have developed preconceived ideas. Children will normally accept that sound can be drawn if they hear tape recordings of sounds such as morse code, for here a line represents a long sound and a dot a short sound. Music, too, can be interpreted by drawn symbols. A soft melody is likely to be shown by an undulating line, a short, fast-moving rhythm is likely to become a zigzag line. The use of texture to depict sound is not really unfamiliar to children, as comic cartoon illustrators frequently represent motion and noise by texture.

Once a grammar of symbols peculiar to each child has been built up, the representation of more complicated sounds should be possible. Screeching of brakes, explosions, breaking glass, wood being sawn, can all be interpreted in either paint or other two-dimensional media. A tape-recorder will prove a great asset with this kind of work.

30a   Photogram of grasses and seed pods

PLATE 2   *Painting of an aquarium by a*
five-year-old

Photographic aids

The use of cameras to record textures can be a most valuable aid in and out of the classroom. The development of *Polaroid* cameras which can produce finished photographs within seconds of picture-taking, both in black and white and in colour, would have obvious advantages in the recording of textural objects not easily removed from their environment. Cameras, however, can be expensive items, but this should not exclude the use of simple photographic means to produce textural effects. Transparency holders, for 35 mm films, are obtainable from most photographic shops. They consist of a plastic frame which supports two sheets of glass. It is possible to trap delicate parts of natural forms between the sheets of glass and with the use of a projector simple objects will take on a new identity. Petals of flowers, leaves, thin grasses, all can prove to be the most exciting objects when thus magnified. Coloured inks and dyes freely used can also provide interesting textures. Children will often need to evolve new tools to enable them to manipulate the media and will use things like pins, drinking straws and match sticks as well as brushes to apply the designs.

Photograms are easy to produce, providing a dark cupboard is available. All that is required is a 'safe' light, photographic enlarging paper, bromide paper is probably the most useful, a dish to contain developer and also a dish for the fixer, and a sink or bucket of water to wash the prints. A light source is also required, but this can be very simple and a 25 Watt bulb suspended one foot from the paper will give a maximum exposure time of about 5 seconds. The working technique is simple: objects are placed on the bromide paper, eg drawing pins (thumbtacks), a light source is switched on for one second, then off. The objects are then moved slightly and the light switched on again for a second and then off, and the process is repeated, if required, for a total of 5 seconds, which should give a reasonable range of tone. However, experimentation may be necessary to establish the requirements under particular conditions. The paper should then be developed until a satisfactory tone range is achieved and then placed in the fixer for approximately ten minutes and washed for about half an hour in water. The most exciting results can be produced from found objects. One group of primary school children produced most beautiful photograms from a dead bird. Objects found in the classroom, for example paper clips, coins, pen-nibs, staples, all produce excellent results. This technique is by no means new as direct contact methods have been known since the beginning of photography in the mid-nineteenth century.

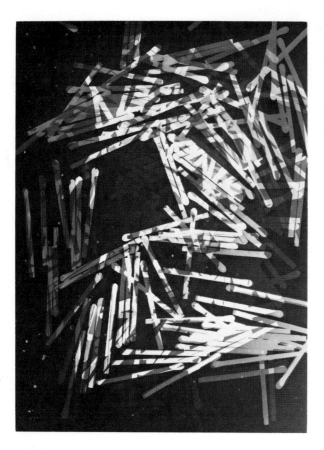

Possible lines of development

Collection of objects and classification into textural quality of variable surfaces.

Display tables of contrasting qualities.

TWO-DIMENSIONAL QUALITIES
Varying qualities of paint and marks from various media.

Paint on various surfaces: rough, smooth, hard, soft, etc.

Rubbings.

Simple print making.

Texture created from dye-stuffs. Batik, Tie-dye.

Use of cameras. *Polaroid*, 35 mm, photograms.

Projection of textures. 50 × 50 mm slides made up from various media and parts of natural objects.

THREE-DIMENSIONAL EXPERIENCES
Raised surfaces on paper: pin-pricks, cut, torn, etc.

Use of clay and other materials: pressure, subtraction and addition.

The creation of pleasant and unpleasant surfaces.

Collage.

30b   Photogram of match sticks

*31   A four-year-old experimenting with hand
prints*

32 *Student teachers working on a Christmas*
decoration using tie and dye and block printing

Part 2   The implication of time in children's work

Innate ability

The Oxford Dictionary defines motion as 'a moving change of place'. Certainly any change in the environment receives quick responses from both men and animals whose survival may well depend on their reactions. A fish will dart away if it detects movement on the river bank and birds and animals will remain still or take to flight if they become aware of unusual movement.

Movement can also be pleasurable; young animals love to play with things, although this too may be play for a purpose. Babies like dangling toys and young children enjoy games that involve movement – skipping, blowing bubbles, playing with a balloon or kite, or just watching the sea. Fair grounds with their swings and roundabouts illustrate our love of involvement with movement.

Man and animals are sensitive to conditions of change even before they can identify the object that causes it, their eyes are adapted to the environment in which they live and have to respond. However, our eyes have a limited range of detection and our perception is experience

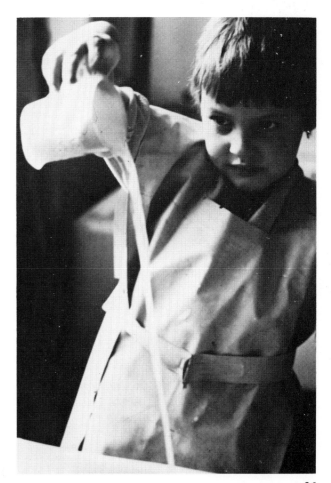

33   A child enjoying the sensation of pouring liquid

intelligence, emotion personality and culture. Although we become so used to seeing things that we pay little attention to them, movement is perhaps the aspect we perceive most readily and most normally react to because of its attraction and warning of possible dangers.

Motion can be divided into three kinds: (1) that which is observed; (2) that in which a person is involved, and (3) that which is represented in art forms, for example, watching someone on a swing or participating in swinging, or producing a picture or sculpture of someone swinging.

All these kinds of motion can be involved in visual education and the area is so rich in exciting new stimuli that the possibilities are almost endless.

Toy manufacturers are sensitive to the needs of children, and toys are available in simple and in complex forms, from the push and pull variety, gravity or wind driven, to the sophisticated electrically propelled kind. Water play and sand play, as well as being tactile experiences, are also kinetic. It could be possible that hidden amongst the commonplace play activities and playthings of children – paper aeroplanes, kites, bubbles, balloons and wind-mills – are the beginnings of new and vital experiences which could open up fresh understanding of the environment.

34 ABOVE *Baby and kitten are both attracted by the movement of string*

35 BELOW *The floating movement of bubbles are a constant attraction to children*

Early kinetic experiences

It is impossible to isolate the early tactile experiences of young children from that of motion. Scribble is an experience of muscular co-ordination and as such an experience which must involve movement through the manipulation of arms, wrists and fingers. The various types of scribble, from the uncontrolled varieties to the controlled, are in fact a graphic representation of the movement involved in producing them.

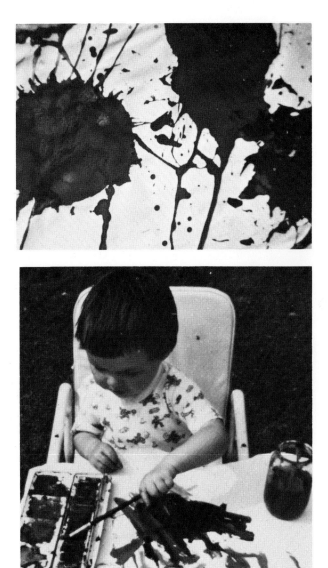

36 ABOVE *Blow painting*

37 BELOW *Uncontrolled scribble by child of twenty months*

Time sequence in children's drawings

Motion is inseparable from time. One cannot exist without the other. Time sequence will often appear in the drawings of young children. Sometimes they take the form of a progression of images, rather like the Bayeaux Tapestry. This form of drawing probably owes much to the influence of comic papers where a progression of pictures reveals the adventures of a character. Another or similar process of time sequence usually involves the repetition within a picture of a figure. The figure, often the 'self' figure, can be seen both watching the television and also in bed upstairs, the whole drawing being revealed through the wall of a house as though the wall were transparent. Viktor Lowenfeld refers to this as X-ray drawing in his book *Creative and Mental Growth*.

In their eagerness to express an idea on paper, children will occasionally express motion through the very speed of the execution of the work, for example the whirl of a circular line to indicate the action of a piece of machinery. Here the movement involved is very similar to that of action painting.

With very young children, during the period of symbolism, the use of a multiple image frequently appears in their drawings of animals, where the legs of an animal may be represented many times. This may be linked with a lack of number concept, but it is possible that it could also be associated with the complexity of viewing a quickly moving animal which could appear to have many legs.

38 ABOVE *Five-year-old's version of an accident*

39 BELOW *Eleven-year-old's version of an accident*

40 *Painting by a five-year-old of a little girl crying; the running paint stimulated the idea in the child's mind*

41 ABOVE *Painting of an elephant with eleven legs by a four-year-old*

42 BELOW *Children should be encouraged to study objects that move*

Apparent motion

The use of a progression of drawings may make a valuable contribution to the extension of a child's visual vocabulary. Children may be asked to describe in simple visual terms an action like cleaning their teeth, or washing their faces. Consideration, of course, must be given to the age of the child, and to his or her command of visual shapes, and care should be taken not to set problems which are too complicated.

Where repetition is required, cut paper or print making with a potato or lino can prove to be most helpful and avoid difficult or monotonous repetition with a brush. The repeated image of a falling leaf, a bouncing ball or a bubble floating can be expressed more easily by a simple form of printing. With the older children in the school, the expression of the action and function of a simple tool, for example, a pair of scissors or a hammer, can be beneficial to their visual expression. The movement in a clock, though very complicated, can be an exciting experience for children to interpret.

The actual involvement in motion by children climbing or swinging on apparatus could certainly stimulate those children who are subjective in their approach to creative work and there are obvious links which could be established with the art of movement and drama activities in the school curriculum.

Actual motion

Most of the previous experiences have been two-dimensional and the use of three-dimensional experiences is important to keep a well-balanced curriculum. An opportunity should always be given for the children to explore both areas. With large classes, division into groups is helpful and the interplay of ideas is beneficial.

Children should be encouraged to study objects that move – the egg-whisk, games like bagatelle, spinning coins, and tops. Descriptions of these should be verbal or written as well as drawn or painted, and tape recordings made of the sound of both fast and slow moving objects.

A simple exercise of marking a cardboard disc which is about 100 mm (4 in.) in diameter with a dot and spinning it on a string will allow a child the opportunity of discovering that the dot turns into a line when motion is applied. This kind of discovery can lead to more complex problems and involve tone, colour and various geometric shapes. This, too, could lead on to the production of flick books where an action or simple story, for example the dancing broom in *The Sorcerer's Apprentice*, could have implied motion. Much could be borrowed from the ingenious inventions of the nineteenth century where static images were given implied motion by machines like the zoetrope or the phenokistoscope.

*43   Children should also be encouraged to study
objects with which they can create movement*

45 *Creating shapes that move by wind pressure. Here a boy has discovered that by blowing through a straw he can induce movement in the propellor*

44 *Designing shapes that fly*

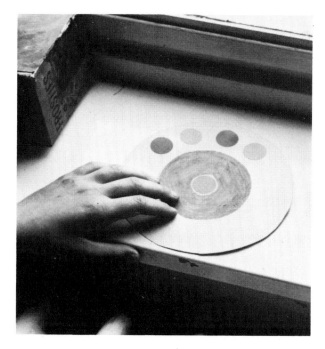

46 *Preparation of a disc to discover the effect of movement on spots of colour. Work carried out by seven-year-olds*

47 *Observation of changes in lines by spinning a disc*

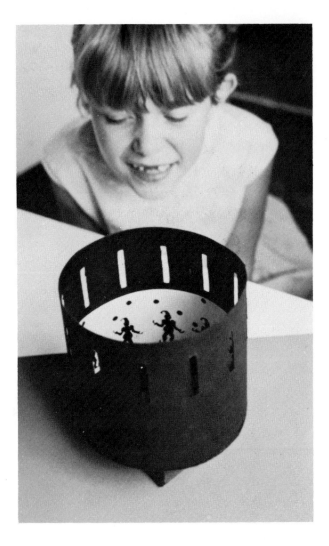

48   *Zoetrope. A nineteenth century device made
in cardboard by a student teacher as a visual
aid. The images inside the cylinder should be
viewed through the slots when the cylinder is spun
giving implied motion*

42

Clues of motion in pictures

Action can be implied if images are presented in a particular way, for example an umbrella inside out, the smoke from a chimney drawn in a horizontal manner, or a tree bent over. From these images we would deduce that it is windy. This conclusion comes from these images together with our knowledge which has been built up from our observations of such happenings in the world in which we live.

Children can be encouraged to discover for themselves what happens to smoke when the wind blows, or the movement of clothes on a clothes line. It must be accepted that the presentation of visual clues of this kind will depend very much on the knowledge of the child, and may frequently be stereotyped and stiff, but this should not deter encouragement for this kind of observation and discovery, and it should be equally acceptable in discussions and in written form. Each child should check the problem at his own level, the more advanced children studying the differences of the effect of different strengths of wind upon, for example, a lake or river, or compare how the motion of rain differs from that of snow, or study the rising flight of the skylark with its descending flight, and find out what happens to a wheel when it turns round at various speeds.

49   Use of line by a six-year-old to imply motion in smoke blowing

50   Potato print of cockerels fighting by eleven-year-old boys

PLATE 3 Green and Red Policeman *by a four-year-old*

Change of identity

Time can create a change of identity in material things: for example the rotting of an old building or a piece of wood, or the erosion of rock. The growth of a bud to a leaf or a seed to a plant is another form of time creating a change of shape. The link here between science and art is very close and the search that children have to make very similar, for both are concerned with finding and discovering something about these changes. Burning produces change, and (with of course the utmost precaution against fire) a teacher could demonstrate the change of character that occurs when a match is lit and allowed to burn. Drawings and photographs can be made at particular points during the various stages that occur. Projects could be set for children to discover how time has changed things in their locality.

Vocabulary based on motion and time

Children should be encouraged to build up a display corner in the classroom based on movement. Words associated with the objects, models or photographs presented should be used to label them. The words chosen will, of course, depend upon the age of the children involved in the exercise. Use of a dictionary or, with the older children, Roget's *Thesaurus*, could prove to be very helpful. Simple topics involving 'self' would be more suitable for very young children: words like walking, running, stepping, striding, sliding, eating, climbing, falling, quickly and slowly. Words can be directed to describe a particular element in the environment, for example, water – spurting, squirting, spouting, splashing,

51   Explosions. Wax crayon and water colour

45

rushing, gushing, falling, cascading; or rain – gently falling, downpouring, driving, pouring, drenching. More imaginative words could follow like diving, zooming, spinning, hovering, flowing and flying. Words associated with forces or pressures are pushing, thrusting, jolting, hurtling, hitting, breaking, tearing, twisting, crushing, crashing, smashing. Objects which rise can be grouped together, for example, bubbles, balloons, rockets, aeroplanes and birds. The displays should include photographs of people, animals, transport and the elements associated with some of the words mentioned.

Imaginative approach

Moving forces which are dynamic, powerful and violent appeal to young children, particularly boys. Such things are exciting. The children quickly react to suggestions of topics involving them and usually highly imaginative paintings and drawings result. The possibilities are endless, but suggestions such as an earthquake, a volcano, the end of the world (see plate 3), fire, explosions, all these terms will produce a healthy and total involvement. A tape-recorder could prove to be an added incentive to work and the sounds of racing engines, shattering glass or a combination of sounds could help to stimulate and excite a class. At one school, paintings and drawings of this kind were photographed on 35 mm film and the slides combined with synchronised tape-recordings, which produced an effective project in itself.

Movement of the observer

When we examine an apple we involve motion. We turn the apple round in our hands and look at it from different angles. When we look at a painting, our movement is much more simple and we move forwards or backwards from the painting. Artists such as Yacoov Agam have sought ways to produce more interesting possibilities in the viewing of a two-dimensional work. The corrugation of the surface has been one answer. Here a painting may appear to be totally different when approached from the left than it does when approached from the right, but from the front the two designs become resolved. So as a person walks past the painting, it will change in composition.

Moiré, the word used to describe the peculiar shimmering patterns that appear when silk is laid over silk, can also be used to produce new images by the change of position of the person viewing them. This peculiar effect occurs sometimes when someone wears a striped dress on television. What happens is this: similar sets of parallel lines are superimposed and the spaces between them become blurred and magnification can take place in these open areas. The designs that result often change identity completely and although it is possible to buy ready-made moiré kits to produce these designs, with reasonably intelligent children it is possible through discovery methods to produce quite effective moiré patterns. These in fact often occur in mathematical models with nylon threads crossed over them at an angle of about 30° or less. Care should be taken, however, to ensure that the children have materials which aid them in their search. There are many published works on this subject and it is an area worthy of exploration, although with the less able children it should be avoided.

Corrugation is a much more simple process and even corrugated card will produce variations of design when viewed from the left or the right.

Mobiles

The first mobile was produced by Alexander Calder in about 1926. It took the form of a suspended sculpture which was free-moving, dependent for its motion on the flow of air. Since this time mobiles have become more common and are frequently used for advertising purposes. They are simple to produce and can be made from the cheapest materials. Their production will involve children in the study of balance and shape relationships as well as movement.

52 *Corrugation by a student teacher. When approached from the left the composition is made up of straight lines and when approached from the right curved lines*

53 *Moiré effect from superimposed circles*

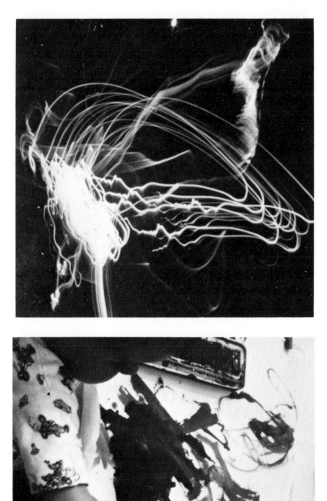

54, 55, and 56   *Spider's web, explosion of a firework and uncontrolled scribble, which are all diagrams of the movement and force that created them*

Summary and possible lines of development

TWO-DIMENSIONAL EXPERIENCES

Early scribble experiences, uncontrolled and controlled. These are instinctive movements but later movement could be encouraged through paintings and could involve body movements, arm movements, finger movements. The result will depend upon these three things:

1 the movement involved,
2 the speed of the movement, and
3 the length of the pause.

The media and the equipment used will also have an effect.

Blow paintings. Patterns created by blowing at paint through a straw.

Paintings on corrugated cardboard presenting various viewpoints.

Paintings and images based on the sound of motion.

Paintings based on subjects that inspire the use of symbolic clues, for example, storm, windy day, earthquake, waterfall, machinery.

Observations of movement in the world around us:
Objects and things that move slowly
Objects and things that move quickly
Objects and things that rise in the air
Objects and things that fall
The elements: rain, snow, wind, water, fire.

The influence of time on objects creating change:
Erosion of materials
Disintegration of materials
Rotting of materials
Rusting of materials
Changes in plants through growth.

Observations in the classroom.
Toys and games that involve movement.
Displays dealing with a particular aspect of motion, for example, objects that rise; photographs supported by vocabulary illustrating soap bubbles, birds, aircraft, rockets.

Observations on designs drawn by children on spinning discs in dots, in line and using colour.

The involvement of actual and apparent motion.
Flick-books, leading to designs implying motion, for example, zoetropes, mobiles, paper aeroplanes, kites, puppets.

Part 3   The implication of space in children's work

From the time they are a few months old, children are aware of space. They have an innate desire to explore and discover all its aspects. As they grow older, they like to conquer it by running across it, climbing over it or crawling through it, and they enjoy the security offered by being enclosed by it.

Space can be exciting, space can be a self-imposed restriction or a complete freedom. Children love to find space and to use it.

Two-dimensional aspects of space

The earliest marks made by the very young children do not reveal any spatial qualities in the daubs or lines produced. It is possible that some of the adult concepts of space, for example overlapping, perspective, size relationships of known objects, and transparency, may be present in the work of young children by chance, but care should be taken not to come to any hasty conclusions concerning the understanding of a particular spatial concept.

57   Stone's natural veining revealing the contour of the stone

Further developments of two-dimensional work

With the emergence of generalised images or symbols, spatial relationships are still very vague and usually these early works reveal a lack of understanding of relationships of the positions of various objects.

Filling in the linear areas with colour may be the first crude indication of an awareness of space.

The interpretation of three-dimensional objects, which adults are conditioned to present or interpret by use of perspective and representative form, gives children few problems. The difficulties, if they occur, occur in the preconceived ideas of the teacher as each normal child discovers his own way of finding a graphic solution to the problems presented and usually responds to the most dominant aspects, which may simply be the flatness of the paper or the most significant aspect of the stimuli. The drawing of a street with houses on each side of the road, for example, is normally solved by folding the houses down flat. Mixed viewpoints are common and logical and children will frequently show a plan and an elevation in the same drawing.

The bottom edge of the paper is often used as a ground line and as the child's awareness of space develops so the images gradually move up the paper and the relationship of one symbol or shape with another begins to have more importance.

58 *Early two-dimensional work reveals a lack of understanding in the relationships of shapes. The picture is of a baby in a pram painted by a four-year-old*

59 *Street scene by a seven-year-old child, showing both sides of the street. Mixed view points of this kind are common in the work of children of this age*

Transparency (cut-away, section drawings)

The use of transparency to reveal the interior of an object or structure at the same time as its exterior is common and logical. This method is frequently used in technical drawings by adults to show, for example, the workings of engine parts. In the drawings of young children it reveals the eagerness of the child to show the important things that he knows are happening in an enclosed space.

60 *The use of a cut-away section to reveal the interior and exterior of an object at the same time is common and logical*

61 *Cut-away view of a boat sailing under a bridge*

Constructional play

When children are playing with bricks or blocks and constructional toys, they are also enriching their understanding of spatial problems. A plentiful supply of bricks or blocks, boxes, constructional toys of all sizes are an essential to any infant classroom.

The use of drinking straws, cocktail sticks, matchboxes, nuts and bolts, paper clips and other readily available units can form excellent material for spatial constructions. Children can be asked to create the tallest building that they can, or the longest, or even the smallest.

62   A plentiful supply of a variety of materials is essential to any infant classroom

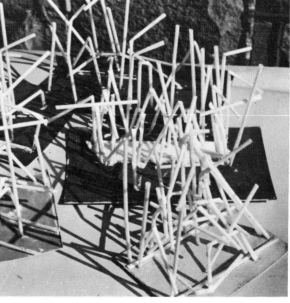

63 ABOVE LEFT *Playing with bricks is also playing with space*

64 ABOVE RIGHT *An exercise in space with a constructional toy*

65 BELOW RIGHT *Simple spatial problem with a limited number of drinking straws*

Recognition of shapes

Recognition and awareness of shapes should form an important part of space discovery and an excellent link with early mathematics. Children should be encouraged to find shapes in their environment and to name the shapes, which will help to extend their vocabulary.

A search could be made for shapes in the classroom, for example:

1   The shape of the room
2   Shapes of the windows
3   Shapes of and in tables and chairs
4   Shapes of books
5   Shapes of equipment used for physical education and crafts etc.

Work cards could be made out to help a search for shapes in the environment, for example:

1   Find a shape you like
2   Find a shape you don't like
3   Visit the grocery store or the supermarket and find out how many shapes you can name
4   How many shapes are there in a car, a bus or a bicycle?
5   How many shapes can you find from the objects in your pockets?

Children should be encouraged to collect shapes and to make up a table of the shapes found in the classroom. Buttons and sweets (candies) are excellent both for their shape and for their link with colour, particularly liquorice allsorts, (candy coated licorice drops) etc.

66   Recognition and awareness of shapes forms an excellent link with mathematics

*67   Chimneys at York University create
beautiful shapes in space*

68　*A superb design within a circle in this Gothic window which could form part of a collection of beautiful shapes*

69　*Intricate shapes in stone at York Minster*

Shapes that fit together

Once children are capable of producing their own shapes either by drawing or by cutting them out from coloured paper, they should be led to discover that certain shapes will fit together and others will not. A circle cut from or torn off a rectangular piece of paper could be used in a positive/negative composition and immediate relationships between the two pieces of paper are obvious. Where simple repetition of shapes may be necessary, print making techniques could be helpful, for example, potato printing, paper printing, cardboard printing and the use of photogram techniques previously described. A search of the environment will soon produce found objects that fit together, for example, nuts and bolts, a ballpoint pen and cap, the two parts of the telephone, cog wheels, an egg and egg-cup.

However, it is not always necessary to leave the classroom to discover shapes that fit together and a beginning may be made by examining a child's clothing – examples like hand and glove, foot and shoe, would be most helpful in establishing the concept.

Various seasons of the year will produce natural shapes that fit together. In autumn, a chestnut and its case are a beautiful example.

The sorting and classification of these objects is an essential part of this exercise, and should help to spark off many developments in two-dimensional and three-dimensional work. Early three-dimensional exercises could be the fitting of boxes one inside another, various shapes in holes which can be found in many constructional toys, and this could lead on to more creative approaches where the children could be encouraged to use clay or plasticine to make their own shapes that fit together.

70 *Shapes that fit together linking art with geometry*

Environments

Children love to hide under bedclothes and produce a space which is their own. The under-side of a table or chair produces the same kind of personal space structure and excitement. Older children build camps in gardens or on waste land (vacant lots) in the cities. These can be ingenious structures made from boxes, planks and branches. They can become aeroplanes, ships, cars, houses or just places to be in.

The playhouse, known as a Wendy House, in Great Britain, still exists in many reception classrooms and is usually in great demand for young children but these structures are often too limited and rigid in design. There are much more exciting and simple ways of creating flexible structures which can be explored by both very young and older children. All that is required is a corner of a room, space in a corridor or a small part of the school playground or playing field. Fabric or scrim pinned to a wall and stretched out and pinned to the floor can produce a very simple and effective structure, as can the under-side of a chair or table. The colouring of the fabric by spray or tie-dye can enhance the appearance. Children will enjoy the interior and exterior problems in constructing a house. The naming of the various parts or rooms will be a useful extension to the child's vocabulary. Measurement can also play an important part. Dance and drama can be involved at a latter stage in the use of the house or of a created environment.

Environments can be made to look at, to look into and to be played with or in. They can be produced from anything – from something as small as a matchbox to something as large as a packing case. In the environment produced in a matchbox, the small scale is the problem. Environments which are made from, perhaps, shoeboxes, and which can be peered into from peepholes, are perhaps more satisfactory. Then the subject matter can be based on anything from a treasure cave to strange objects on an unknown planet. Light could be filtered through coloured gelatines, acetate or cellophane papers, and this could form a link with the understanding of colour.

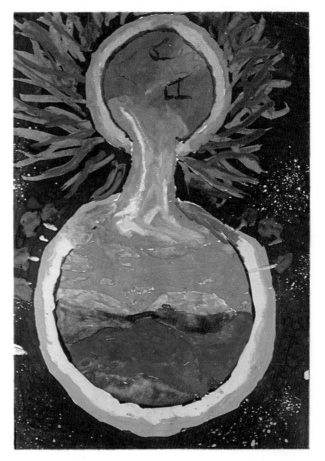

PLATE 4   Rocket Ascending *by a ten-year-old*   The End of the World *by a ten-year-old*

71 and 72   Dealing with a spatial problem
within the limitations of a box

At Easter time an egg form would be a topical and interesting structure to create, large enough for one or two children to get inside. Or, with the recent advances into space exploration, models of lunar modules would be an excellent idea for a structural environment.

73 and 74   Space exploration stimulates the use of boxes to create a simple environmental structure

Although tea-chests or various kinds of boxes would form the normal components, interesting environments can also be produced from hanging materials such as different coloured wools, ropes, strings, cardboard tubes and coloured ribbons, and these could be used as a basis to stimulate creative writing and dance.

The relationships of various sizes of objects would have obvious links with mathematics. The three bears might form an interesting topic, as the story contains variations in scale, for example, a large chair, a medium chair and a small chair.

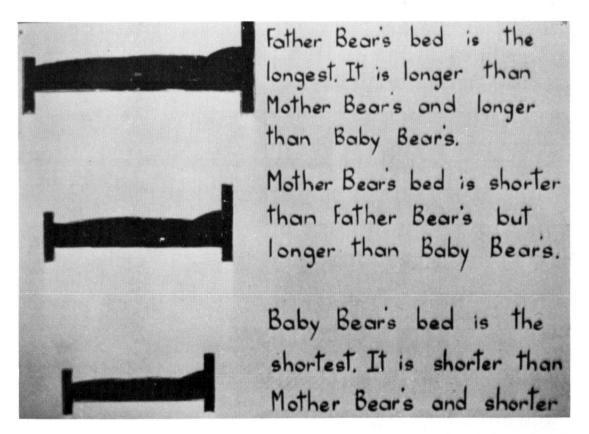

Father Bear's bed is the longest. It is longer than Mother Bear's and longer than Baby Bear's.

Mother Bear's bed is shorter than Father Bear's but longer than Baby Bear's.

Baby Bear's bed is the shortest. It is shorter than Mother Bear's and shorter

75 (ABOVE), 76 and 77 (OVERLEAF)   The relationship of various sizes of objects resulted in using the story of the three bears

r Bear's chair is the
est. It is higher than Mother
r's and higher than Baby
r's.

her Bear's chair is lower
n Father Bear's but higher
n Baby Bears.

by Bear's chair is the
est. It .... Mother
.... her
ar's

father Bear's bowl holds the ..
porridge It holds more porridge
than Mother Bear's bowl and mor
than Baby Bear's bowl.

Mother Bear's bowl holds less
porridge than Father Bear's bow
but more than Baby Bear's bowl

Baby Bear's bowl holds the lea
.... It holds less porridg
.... her Bear's bowl and
.... Father ...... bowl.

78   *Size relationship. David and Goliath. Mural
produced by six and seven-year-olds in torn
paper and water paints*

Possible areas of development

CONSTRUCTIONAL PLAY

Sorting and classifying shapes from junk, displays, etc.

Using the work card method to study shapes in the environment.

Collection of shapes from the environment.

Children should be given an opportunity to produce spatial results in two-dimensional work.

Presuming X-ray vision, they could be encouraged to draw objects with hidden but important interiors.

Special constructions in three-dimensions with units, eg paper-clips, nuts and bolts, straws, matchsticks, etc.

Create environments that can be looked at or looked into or played in.

Search for shapes that go together – found objects, for example, egg and egg-cup, nut and bolt, jig-saws, chestnut and case.

Produce shapes that go together in clay, inspired by the shapes that have been found in nature, for example the chestnut, or in museums, for example helmets and armour, bones, etc.

EMOTIONAL SHAPES

Shapes I like and shapes I don't like, produced in two - and three-dimensions.

Construct imaginary animals from found shapes – and this of course can be extended into puppetry.
Hanging shapes, mobiles, etc.

Part 4   Light and colour

When sunlight passes through a prism it produces a band of colours like the colours we see in a rainbow. The colours range from red to violet. A great deal has been written on their physical properties but a great deal of confusion can arise between understanding the colour in light and the colour in pigment. An artist normally deals with the problems concerning colour in paint.

Sir Isaac Newton discovered relationships between the colours of the spectrum. He placed these round a circle in the order that he found them; this is known as a natural order. He was able to include the purples and the reds not found in the spectrum. He discovered that the colours opposite each other in the circle had a peculiar effect on each other, and these were called *complementary colours*. Artists can play many tricks with complementary colours. If fluorescent yellow paint is used on a white board, the opposite or complementary colour, in this case violet, will appear like magic on the white ground. Psychologists call this the *after-image*. When complementary colours are placed together in a painting, the colour appears to jump and to vibrate.

The most important colours are red, yellow and blue, as all the other colours can be made from these three. These colours are called the *primary colours*. When two primary colours are mixed, the colour that results is known as a secondary colour. For example, blue mixed with yellow will give a secondary colour, green. Yellow mixed with red will give the secondary colour, orange.

Colour can be talked about in terms of tone, tint and shade. The *tone* of a colour is the lightness and the darkness of the colour. The tint of a colour is the lightness of the colour created by adding white. The *shade* of a colour is the darkness of the colour made by adding black. The *hue* of a colour has several meanings but the most common is when the colour is referred to rather than the tone.

Artists often talk of warm colours and cool colours. The warmest colours are normally on the top end of the colour circle (the reds, oranges, yellows, and yellow greens) and the coldest colours are normally found at the bottom half of the circle (the blues, violets, and blue-greens).

Colour theory is not necessary when working with very young children and it may be regarded as being out of place in a book of this kind. It is, however, important that anyone teaching colour to children should have some knowledge of the simplest theory.

A good deal of research has been carried out on the understanding and significance of colour in the graphic representations of young children but much still needs to be done before really reliable data is available.

By general opinion, the early selection of colour by young children is emotional and often the selection of a particular colour would appear to be entirely on impulse. Children tend to respond to the brighter colours, reds, oranges, etc, and as they get older they tend to use the blues and greens, but it is dangerous to generalise about this.

Children who may be abnormal in some way may only use black and white or very sombre colours. The understanding of the use of colour often runs parallel to the understanding and use of line. The emotional use of colour is frequently revealed in the work of very young children. One little girl produced a bright green policeman (see plate 4), although when questioned she was quite aware of the actual colour of a policeman's uniform, but she just liked green policemen!

The next stage of development is the generalised presentation of colour to represent certain objects in the environment, for example, all roads are black, all skies are blue, all grass is green, all houses are red.

Some of the children in our class have got Measles.

79   *Early use of colour is normally by chance*

80   *Measles is the subject uppermost in the child's mind and therefore becomes the most important feature of this painting by a six-year-old*

Light and colour

Without light, colour cannot exist, and children should be shown by being deprived of light that colour is completely dependent on it. This is certainly not the case in the recognition of texture or form or shape, which can be recognised by touch alone.

Light, depending on its strength, will affect the intensity of the colour. In the early morning when conditions are misty and the sunlight is very weak, trees and the landscape generally take on a very different colour from their appearance on a bright, sunny mid-day. Children should be shown the various effects of the intensity of light on objects by very simple means, for example, different kinds of glass could be used to filter the light, but simpler still, a large cardboard box into which a child could crawl, the entrance of which could be covered by a cloth or a flap and the light through the windows controlled by coloured gelatines acetate or cellophane paper, would be quite effective.

Explanation as to why the filters work will come later when the children are older, perhaps in a combined physics and art course, but at this age it is sufficient for the children to observe these happenings.

Reflections

The study of light and colour could lead to an interest in shiny or reflective surfaces. Certainly people generally appear to enjoy having highly reflective substances about them, from the sparkle of precious stones to the reflective metals and paints used on motor cars, and the tinsel, glitter and coloured globes which are so familiar at Christmas time. Children could be encouraged to collect reflective materials, for example, silver papers, new reflective plastics, metals and mirrors.

Reflections in nature could be studied and noted, or better still, photographed. These will be found in lakes and puddles and also in not so obvious places like wet paving stones. The various changes in the image made by ripples or the distortion of a surface could be noted.

Man-made objects with surfaces that reflect could also be searched for. Some of these have already been mentioned, but there are many others.

After searches of this kind, children should be stimulated sufficiently for them to produce simple structures using reflective materials, for example, cheap mirrors, reflecting ping-pong balls, marbles or dowelling.

Highly reflective plastics that are easily distorted could be great fun and excite much interest.

81 *Reflections created by distorted melimex*

*82, 83 and 84   Simple experiments with a
concave shaving mirror, marbles and a
constructional toy*

85　*Reflective surfaces are very common at Christmas time*

73

86 *Children were asked to tear out particular
colours from magazines and these became
collages*

74

Matching and comparison of colour

The most important piece of equipment at this very early stage is a box of brightly coloured objects. These objects could be coloured plastic, ribbons, fabrics, buttons, beads, etc. Children will enjoy exploring the contents of such a box. Once the novel experience has worn off, the next stage should be to encourage children to sort the various colours, for example:

1 Find the colours you like
2 Find the colour you don't like
3 Put all the same colours together.

Children should be encouraged to write the names of the various colours or, if they lack the ability to write, they should be encouraged to describe the colours in words. Many children will discover that some colours are brighter than others. They may discover a pale blue and a dark blue. This may be an indication that a particular child is ready for a more demanding problem. A box containing tonal variations of one colour can be explored and the child can be asked to place the colours in order from the darkest blue to the lightest blue.

As children become older and more skilled with this kind of sorting, the selection could be made more critical, but care should be taken not to make the range of colours too wide as even some adults find this kind of selection difficult.

Colour collections

Children should be encouraged to collect colours and make up a 'colour corner' in the classroom. The colours could represent a particular season of the year, or simply a particular colour. Toys, photographs, natural and man-made objects could form part of the collection. A pair of old sun-glasses with substituted coloured acetate lenses or coloured cellophane could be available by the colour display to enable the children to see the changes of colour; for example, a yellow group seen through blue glasses will turn green. Coloured spot-lights could also be used to change the colours and the children should be encouraged to talk and write about the various changes that take place.

Two-dimensional aspects

It is strongly recommended that children experiment with colour and find out as much as possible about colour in their environment. The use of graphs could make the children more aware of the most popular colours of clothes in the classroom or cars passing the school, or even flowers in a school garden. Work cards could be made out which might include the following:

1 How many colours in the grocery store's window?
2 Name these colours
3 What is the colour of your house?
   (*a*) windows
   (*b*) doors
   (*c*) brickwork
   (*d*) roof.
4 How many colours are there in your room?
5 Name the colours.

Older children should be encouraged to take one of the primary colours – red, yellow or blue – and mix as many colours as they can from that one colour added to any other colour. Patches of colour would be quite adequate. Younger children could be encouraged to find out how many similar colours they could find by tearing out parts of pictures in magazines. One group could be asked to find all the blues, another greens, another yellows and so on. Again with older children it would be possible for them to find out how many greys they could produce by adding black to white and then to try and find out how many blues they could produce by adding white and black to blue. A more imaginative approach might be to encourage children to paint a picture of an imaginary planet where the landscape and all the objects in the landscape are of one primary colour, for example red. They could also be asked to paint a 'happy' picture or an 'unhappy' picture.

87   Block graph by six-year-old, designed to draw attention to colour in the environment. The collection of such data, in this case the various colours of cars that pass the school in one hour, is enjoyable for most children and helps to increase interest in colour and has obvious links with mathematics. Similar explorations could be made within the classroom, the colour of clothes for example, could also introduce a child to colour relationships

76

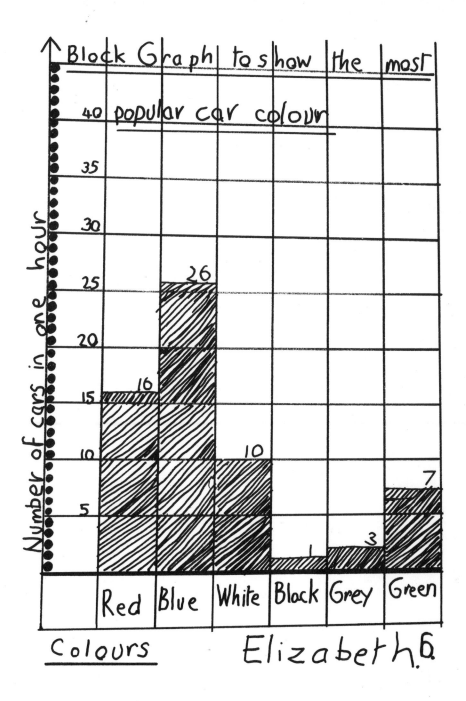

Observations of fireworks and fires usually stimulates exciting pictures in the warmer ranges of colour – reds, yellows and oranges, and these should be encouraged. Again, with older children they could be asked to look at part of a painting by Paul Klee, Van Gogh, Rembrandt or Breughel, and see how many colours they can find in the picture they choose. Younger children should be encouraged to keep a colour scrap-book of all the colours that they like. Colour quizzes could be held to find out who can remember the most colours of places and objects in their school.

Summary and possible lines of development

Sorting and recognition of colour.

Matching of similar colours:
Sweets (candies).
Tearing up magazine pictures and free experiments with paint.

Experiments with intensity of light:
demonstration of light passing through a prism.

Relating tones of colours and producing tonal order.

The use of one colour and black and white to produce a picture, for example, *The Red Planet*, *figure 88*.

Work cards to discover colours in the environment.

Colour graphs to find out the most popular colour in the classroom or of cars passing the school.

Colour corner.

Individual colour collections.

Experiments with transparent material and light, for example free experiments with coloured acetates and the projection of slides decorated with coloured inks.

Vegetable dyeing.

Production of colours from vegetable matter.

Colour games, jig-saws, etc.

A quizz to extend the knowledge of colours.

Structures made from reflective materials.

88   *Paintings by ten-year-olds of imaginary*
planets, using a limited colour scheme, for
example The Red Planet *or* The Green Planet

*89 and 90   Sweets or candies could be a
starting point for sorting and comparing colour*

80

Conclusion

Methods of teaching art vary not only from school to school but from classroom to classroom. This would appear to indicate a flexibility of approach, which is to be complimented, but although the method varies, the products produced may differ only slightly because the attitude is often very similar and owes much to the earlier idealogical origins of 'free expression'. Adult intrusion into such a working atmosphere is often repressed for fear of stemming a subterranean flow of creative ideas. Similar fears also prevent many teachers from forming a structure in their creative activities curriculum, where they tend to favour instead chance methods. Unfortunately many such courses often fade after very exciting beginnings and hardly bear comparison to the more recently produced progressive methods in the sciences.

It would be reasonable to suggest that art like many other subjects possesses a body of knowledge, but this is not to infer that intuition is not a vital part of the creative process, simply that it is only part of the visual educational process and that it must be balanced and not over-weighted in its importance, even though it will be present in every activity.

Most teachers and parents would agree that children should make progress in all aspects of their education, but the identification of such progress in a subject like visual education is difficult. It is possible to refer to developmental scales of the kind proposed by art educators and psychologists. The scales give a specific relationship between the kinds of symbols children draw and their actual ages.

Recent criticism has been levelled at such scales by many teachers on the grounds that chronological age is a poor indicator of actual ability and potential, children are individuals with wide variables. More important, such symbols will depend upon the kind and effectiveness of the teaching the children receive.

Since the turn of the century art teachers have been aware that art education in any form should not be taught by rote learning methods. Many teachers prefer to take an opposite point of view approaching visual education by intuition, feeling what is right or wrong in a particular situation. Experience is really required to aid such a method and it becomes a vital contributor to the process.

It is not a question of opposing such a method, because most teachers use such intuition at one time or another, and it can be of the utmost value, but rather to question the content of what is being taught. Ideally a blending of the intuitive with the more rational approach seems to be a sensible attitude, for both are part of the learning process.

Unfortunately, some teachers tend to oppose any semblance of a rational system on the grounds of its inhibitory effects on free expression. Nothing could be further from the truth and such fears reflect the adult imposed concepts of the nineteenth century.

Such methods are now behind us; we live in an age that has long since accepted the importance of child centred education. Much has happened in psychology in the study of human behaviour, offering to the teacher a wide range of differing points of view to aid the clarification of his theories. A particular example of this kind of clarification may be found in the evidence put forward by psychologists on the concept of creativity. Even though such work is far from complete, the teacher may find much to help him in the identification of the components that make up the concept, either from the point of view of the person, the process or the product, and also in the relationship of creativity to intelligence.

Description of such findings is not possible within the limitations of this book, but access to them is simple. Each teacher must decide for himself the value of such information in relation to his philosophy in visual education.

It could be that such reading may make us aware of blind spots in our thinking and reveal a too narrow or ill defined approach in teaching, or suggest better ways of making progress.

It is said that the only way to discover if learning or progress has been made is by giving some form of test, and that this should show some relatively permanent change in behaviour. This may be true for many subjects, but art is far too complex a subject to be measured in such a way.

We may gain much more from the observation of the children we teach. We may observe the way they work independently and co-operatively, and changes in their behaviour, the development of their ability to respond to differing situations, their flexibility, the methods they use to make their own observations and methods of recording them. The way they express themselves with language, and visually in their paintings and constructions. The way they use their imagination and their ability to be original. The development of skills in techniques of construction and strategies used in handling the various materials.

The teacher will be constantly involved in the various activities, never passive, carefully guiding, helping in the search and allowing the discovery and expression to be made by the child. The guiding and helping of each child to discover does not imply domination, but sympathetic and skilful teaching involving careful planning. It is most important to ensure that each child has the necessary concepts before introducing new information or activities. Lack of interest, the rush to the security of the steroetype or repetitions may be indications that these necessary concepts are not present and a different approach is required.

It is simple to state that the classroom environment should be stimulating and exciting, but this will only emerge through preparation, imagination and hard work. Each teacher must decide the value of having such an environment ready for the class to enter each morning. Such a condition will quickly produce its own feedback in the form of happy and interested children.

The areas chosen in this book for discussion can be introduced to children at any age; the method of introduction will depend only on the ability of the children and the viewpoint of the teacher.

It has not been the intention to propose that children should not enjoy painting and drawing pictures, for such experiences play a vital part in the schemes suggested. Rather it has been stated that such activities should not be repeated day after day with only very limited variations. For limitations of this or any other kind will prevent children from making progress in their understanding or in maintaining a lively interest in the subject. A child's language is first shaped by its mother and a child's relationship to the visual world can be shaped by its parents and teacher.

It is not the intention to propose the more rational approach to visual education contesting it with the experienced teacher's intuition. Rather the aim has been to suggest a blending of the two. This may also apply to the child, when the blending of intuitive play activities with more purposeful activities can lead to the development of his concepts. Thus he finds more pleasure and interest in things shaped by nature or produced by man and is more capable of aesthetic response to the world he perceives.

Bibliography

These books have been selected to extend the understanding of the sections referred to in this book, but the selection is by no means exhaustive. They are also selected to help in the planning of visual educational activities and are grouped under their appropriate headings to aid reference.

General Reading

Draw they must   RICHARD CARLINE
Edward Arnold 1968

Readings in Art Education   E. W. EISNER AND D. ECKER
Blaisdell Publishing Co. 1966

Change in Art Education   DICK FIELD
Routledge and Kegan Paul 1970

Principles of Perceptual Learning and Development
ELEANOR GIBSON   *Appleton Century Crafts 1969*

Creative and Mental Growth   VIKTOR LOWENFELD
Macmillan 1964

Beginnings 1   *Nuffield Mathematics Project 1967*

The Child's Conception of the World   JEAN PIAGET
Routledge and Kegan Paul 1967

Art and Education   MICHAEL STEVENI
Batsford 1968

Tactile and textural experiences

Creative Rubbings   LAYE ANDREW
Batsford 1967

Creative Print Making   PETER GREEN
Batsford 1967

Creative Textile Craft—Thread and Fabric
ROLF HARTUNG   *Batsford 1969*

Creative Corrugated Paper Craft   ROLF HARTUNG
Batsford 1968

Tie and Dye as a Present Day Craft   ANNE MAILE
Mills and Boon 1963

Surfaces in Creative Design   ERNST RÖTTGER
Batsford 1970

Creative Paper Craft   ERNST RÖTTGER
Batsford 1970

Creative Wood Craft   ERNST RÖTTGER
Batsford 1967

Creative Clay Craft   ERNST RÖTTGER
Batsford 1969

Creative Drawing—Point and Line   ERNST RÖTTGER
AND DIETER KLANTE   *Batsford 1969*

Introducing Batik   EVELYN SAMUEL
Batsford 1969

The implication of time in children's work

Nature and Art of Motion   GYORGY KEPES
1965

Vision in Motion   MOHOLY-NAGY
Paul Theobald (Chicago) 1947

The Child's Conception of Time   JEAN PIAGET
Routledge and Kegan Paul 1970

Origins and Development of Kinetic Art   FRANK
POPPER   *Studio Vista 1968*

The Origins of the Motion Picture   D. B. THOMAS
A Science Museum Publication H.M.S.O. 1964

The implication of space in children's work

The Psychology of Children's Drawings   HELGA ENG
Routledge and Kegan Paul 1966

The Nature of Creative Activity   VIKTOR LOWENFELD
Routledge and Kegan Paul 1952

Environmental Geometry   *Nuffield Mathematics
Project 1969*

The Child's Conception of Space   JEAN PIAGET AND
INHELDER BARBEL   *Routledge and Kegan Paul 1967*

The Psychology of Perception   M. D. VERNON
Pelican Original 1962

Light and colour

Lichens for Vegetable Dyeing   EILEEN BOLTON
Studio Books 1960

Colour Matching and Mixing   ALFRED HICKETHIER
Batsford 1970

The New Vision and Abstract of an Artist
MOHOLY-NAGY
George Wittenborn Inc. (New York) Fourth Edition 1947

Shadow Theatres and Shadow Films   LOTTE REINIGER
Batsford 1970

Colour and Form   GOTTFRIED TRITTEN
Batsford 1970

Suppliers

Paints and crayons

George Rowney and Company
10-11 Percy Street
London W 1

Reeves and Sons Limited
Lincoln Road
Enfield, Middlesex

Clifford Milburn Limited
54 Fleet Street
London E C 4

The Morilla Company Inc.
43-01 Twenty-first Street
Long Island City
New York, USA

Stafford-Reeves Inc.
626 Greenwich Street
New York
New York, 10014, USA

The Morilla Company of California
2866 West Seventh Street
Los Angeles,
California, USA

Coloured foils

Art and Crafts Unlimited
49 Shelton Street
London W C 2

Adhesives   (*Marvin Medium*)

Margros Limited
Monument House
Monument Way West
Woking, Surrey

Eagle Pencil Company
Danbury
Connecticut, USA

*Copydex, Evostick, Dufix/Elmer's glue,
Sobo (USA)*
Available from most stationers and hardware stores